AF323592

The Holocaust

T. E. BAXTER
Elementary Library

THE HOLOCAUST

BY MARTIN GITLIN

Content Consultant
Dr. Arnold Krammer, professor of history
Texas A&M University

ABDO
Publishing Company

CREDITS

Published by ABDO Publishing Company, 8000 West 78th Street, Edina, Minnesota 55439. Copyright © 2011 by Abdo Consulting Group, Inc. International copyrights reserved in all countries. No part of this book may be reproduced in any form without written permission from the publisher. The Essential Library™ is a trademark and logo of ABDO Publishing Company.

Printed in the United States of America,
North Mankato, Minnesota
062010
092010

 THIS BOOK CONTAINS AT LEAST 10% RECYCLED MATERIALS.

Editor: Amy Van Zee
Copy Editor: Erin Molta
Interior Design and Production: Becky Daum
Cover Design: Christa Schneider

Library of Congress Cataloging-in-Publication Data
Gitlin, Marty
  The Holocaust / Martin Gitlin.
     p. cm. — (Essential events)
  Includes bibliographical references and index.
  ISBN 978-1-61613-683-3
  1. Holocaust, Jewish (1939-1945)—Juvenile literature. I. Title.
  D804.34.G58 2011
  940.53'18—dc22

                              2010009925

TABLE OF CONTENTS

The manor where the Wannsee Conference was held in 1942

Blueprint
for Mass Murder

It was noon in the German capital of Berlin. In a stately manor in the beautiful suburb of Wannsee, 14 top government officials were about to coordinate horrible crimes against humanity.

The date was January 20, 1942. The guns of World War II had been blasting for more than two years. German dictator Adolf Hitler had already launched an unprovoked and murderous attack against Poland. His armies had since conquered much of Europe, including France, and they had marched deep into the Soviet Union, where they were meeting stiff resistance.

But the men at Wannsee were not there to debate how to win the war. Their goal was to mastermind a plan to kill every one of the 11 million Jewish people in Europe. At the end of the Holocaust, which occurred during World War II, the Nazis had systematically murdered nearly 6 million Jews.

Hitler had promoted a hatred of Jews long before he became chancellor of Germany in 1933. He considered Jewish people to be subhuman and enemies of the country. Soon after he gained power, he proclaimed that Jews should be phased out of society. Hitler and his

Wannsee Conference Villa

The villa just outside of Berlin in which the Wannsee Conference was held is now a Holocaust memorial and education center. It opened in 1992. Four of the 15 rooms in the museum are dedicated to the 1942 meeting itself. Others document Jewish life, the history of Nazism, and the Holocaust.

Germany invaded Poland in 1939. The Polish people were unprepared to fight the advanced German military.

subordinates, including Propaganda Minister Joseph Goebbels, succeeded in convincing millions of people that Jews were going to destroy Germany. Jews were forced to give up their property and belongings for no reason other than their religious beliefs. Others were forcibly removed from their families and taken to concentration camps, where they were punished for crimes they had never committed.

The Nazis also sent other people to the camps—people they saw as political threats or as unworthy of life. Included were Gypsies, the handicapped, Poles, Soviets, communists, homosexuals, and Jehovah's Witnesses.

First, in the 1930s, Jews were banned from many professions, such as law and medicine. In 1935, Jews were inaccurately declared to be a separate race. In reality, Jews did not have biological differences from other Europeans. New laws made it illegal for a German to marry a Jew. Jewish children were forbidden to attend the same schools as other Germans. Many Jews were compelled to leave the country.

The world watched in horror in November 1938 when the German public turned openly against their Jews during Kristallnacht. But the widespread massacre did not begin until Germany conquered Poland

Polish Defense

A stunning example of the superiority of the German army in Poland was seen on the battlefield in September 1939. During that month, Polish forces on horseback faced Germans in powerful tanks. The Germans conquered Poland in just a matter of weeks.

in 1939. Poland was home to 3.5 million Jews, which was more than any other country in Europe. Many were rounded up and forced into cramped ghettos. These were sections of cities where the Jews lived in terrible conditions and were given little food. Some starved to death. Others were selected for hard labor, but many of these laborers died of disease or starvation.

Still, the Jews were not being murdered quickly enough for Hitler and his subordinates, a police force called the Gestapo, and the *Schutzstaffel* (SS). By the end of the war, the very name of the SS struck terror in the hearts and minds of nearly everyone in Europe.

Mass Murder Begins

The SS began its murderous rampage against the Jews in earnest following the invasion of the Soviet Union in June 1941. Troops of

SS men followed the German army, rounding up and killing Jews. But with 11 million Jews from all over Europe as a target, it was decided that a more efficient plan needed to be coordinated.

The 14 men at the Wannsee Conference met to discuss such a plan. SS leader Reinhard Heydrich headed the meeting. He began by presenting a history of the measures already taken to force the Jews out of Germany. He added that Hitler had authorized all Jews in the conquered areas to be sent to eastern European countries for further treatment. Some would be placed into ghettos. Others would be worked to death. The rest would simply be murdered.

The plan to eliminate all the Jews of Europe had been documented as far back as December 1940. That was when Adolf Eichmann, who attended the Wannsee Conference, was in charge of evacuating the occupied areas of Jews. He compiled a report that included the section, "The Final Solution of the Jewish Question."[1] The "Final Solution" came to mean the annihilation of the Jewish "race" in Europe. A secret government medical program in Berlin, called simply the T-4 program, experimented with efficient killing methods.

Few argued with Heydrich that fateful day. The 13 other attendees all agreed that every Jew in Europe, even those tens of thousands of German Jews who had earned medals for bravery as soldiers in World War I, must die.

Heydrich listed the Jewish population figures of each European country. The conversation at Wannsee then drifted into specifics, such as transportation issues and the status of non-Jews who were married to Jews. It was suggested their marriages be forcibly ended and their children sterilized so no others with Jewish blood could be born. The gathering also discussed eliminating Polish Jews as rapidly as possible, which would create room for the rest of the Jews in Europe to be moved east for eventual extermination.

The meeting addressed what to do with those Jews who survived their forced heavy labor. This forced labor included projects such as building roads or making equipment for the German military. Eichmann suggested they be "treated accordingly" to prevent them from forming a "new cell from which the Jewish race could again develop."[2] After the war, Eichmann was put on trial for his crimes. During the trial, he was asked what "treated accordingly" meant. He answered matter-of-factly, "Killed. Killed. Undoubtedly."[3]

Did the Germans Know?

It has been debated how much German civilians were aware of the measures taken to exterminate the Jews. The simple answer is that most Germans were aware that something was happening to their Jewish neighbors.

Moreover, the newspapers were filled with prophecies of doom. For example, a column in the weekly magazine *Volk und Rasse* in May 1942 stated, "A proper understanding of Jews and Judaism

The Trial of Adolf Eichmann

Some Nazis escaped justice following World War II by going into hiding. Adolf Eichmann, who was responsible for deporting millions of Jews to death camps, was almost one of them.

Eichmann fled after the war. He and other Nazis found refuge in Argentina, Egypt, Syria, and Chile. In Argentina, Eichmann changed his name to Ricardo Klement in an attempt to hide his true identity. In May 1960, he was tracked down by Israeli Security Service agents and brought to Israel for trial.

He was charged on 15 counts, including crimes against the Jewish people and crimes against humanity. Dozens of witnesses were brought to the stand to testify against Eichmann, who sat inside a bulletproof glass booth.

During the trial, fellow SS leader Dieter Wisliceny quoted Eichmann as exclaiming, "I will laugh when I leap into the grave because I have the feeling that I have killed 5,000,000 Jews. That gives me great satisfaction and gratification."[4] Eichmann was found guilty and sentenced to death by hanging.

cannot but demand their total annihilation." That same month, Labor Minister Robert Ley was quoted in another popular magazine. He claimed, "The war will end with the extermination of the Jewish race."[5]

The Party daily newspaper *Völkischer Beobachter* declared through its war correspondent, "The rumor has spread among the population that it is the task of the Security Police to exterminate the Jews in the occupied territories. The Jews were assembled in the thousands and shot; beforehand they had to dig their own graves."[6] That was precisely what was happening in the Soviet Union, Poland, Latvia, Lithuania, and Hungary.

How did the civilized country of Germany allow an extremist such as Hitler to gain power? Why did so many Germans accept his anti-Jewish diatribes?

The seeds had been planted more than two decades before the 14 men in Wannsee planned the largest mass murder in modern history.

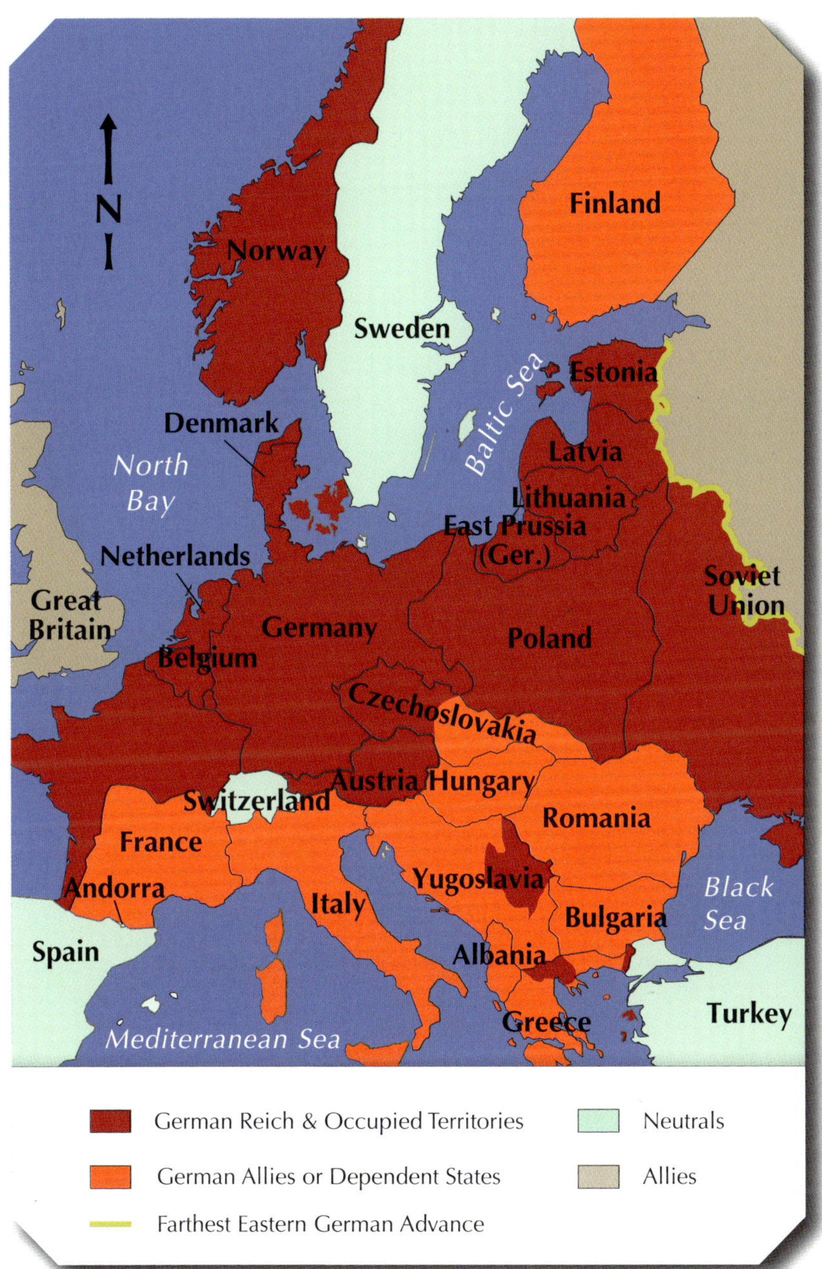

By 1942, German powers had expanded to occupy much of Europe.

Adolf Hitler, front left, with other soldiers during World War I

HITLER, HATRED, PRELUDE TO HORROR

Adolf Hitler was searching for success, but he was not succeeding. He had failed as a student in Linz, Austria. Both his grades and his attitude were poor. In 1907, after high school, he moved to the capital city of Vienna.

He yearned to be an artist but was not talented enough. Angry and miserable, he wandered aimlessly.

But Hitler was not like other vagabonds. He spent hours in the library reading about politics. He read anti-Semitic books and pamphlets. He came to embrace the anti-Jewish sentiment that was prevalent at that time in Austria. His hatred for Jews grew. "Wherever I went," he wrote, "I began to see Jews, and the more I saw, the more sharply they became distinguished in my eyes from the rest of humanity. . . . Later I often grew sick to the stomach from the smell of [Jews]."[1]

It has been speculated that Hitler's anger over his own failures motivated him to target the Jews as a scapegoat. During his four years in Vienna, he would rant about any subject, at any time, to any listener. It was that combination of intense anti-Semitism and his budding talent as a speaker that would eventually transform Germany into a hotbed of hatred.

HITLER'S "SALVATION"

Hitler was a penniless hobo in 1914. He needed an event to spark his life, and World War I was it. Though he was still an Austrian citizen, his request to fight for Germany was granted.

Corporal Hitler fought for the German army in World War I.

Hitler fought with bravery, but his fellow soldiers considered him odd. When the Germans surrendered in 1918, Hitler was devastated. He believed his adopted country had not lost the war on the battlefields. Rather, he thought Jewish traitors had stabbed Germany in the back, despite the thousands of German Jews who fought bravely in the trenches.

His misery grew, and his hatred deepened. By 1919, chaos gripped Germany. Hundreds of new political groups began fighting in the streets. The army's Political Department sent Hitler to spy on the German Workers' Party, a group believed to be dangerous. Hitler was to attend a meeting and report back with the group's plans.

However, Hitler instead decided to join the group himself. The organization preached many of the same views that had been fermenting in his mind, including a strong anti-Jewish philosophy.

Hitler discovered he could influence people. He mesmerized and excited his fellow members with his speeches, and he quickly became the group's unquestioned leader. He changed its name to the National Socialist German Workers' (Nazi) Party.

By the winter of 1920, Hitler had placed anti-Semitism prominently on the Nazi agenda. According to the few hundred Nazi malcontents, Jews were to be denied not only public

The Treaty of Versailles

The anger many Germans felt following World War I was based on the Treaty of Versailles, which ended that conflict in 1918. Because Germany was blamed for starting the war, the terms of the treaty were quite harsh. Among the stipulations was that Germany be almost completely stripped of its military strength. Hitler used the Germans' anger over the Treaty of Versailles to gain favor as well as to recruit members to the Nazi Party.

office in Germany but citizenship as well. Those who had entered the country after 1914 were to be expelled. Though Hitler at the time did not talk specifically about mass murder, he did hint at it. In a speech in the city of Salzburg, Austria, in 1920, he said: "Don't think you can fight racial tuberculosis without taking care to rid the nation of the carrier of that racial tuberculosis." He continued, "This Jewish contamination will not subside, this poisoning of the nation will not end, until the carrier himself, the Jew, has been banished from our midst."[2]

The Jews of Europe

At the time, approximately 500,000 Jews lived in Germany. Other countries in Europe had much larger Jewish populations, including Poland (3.5 million) and the Soviet Union (2.6 million). Though Jews throughout the continent were forced to deal with anti-Semitism, they lived peacefully.

In eastern Europe, most Jews lived in small towns and villages and spoke Yiddish, a language that is similar to German. They tended to be traditional in their clothing and customs. In western European nations such as Germany, Jews had been assimilated into large cities. They lived closely and in harmony with non-Jews, working in fields such as politics, law, medicine, and education. They also dressed the same as non-Jews.

None of that mattered to Hitler and the growing number of anti-Semites in

Not Just in Germany

European Jews had been confronted with violent anti-Semitism for centuries before the Holocaust. During one eight-year period in seventeenth-century Russia, more than 100,000 Jews were murdered. Between 1918 and 1922, approximately 150,000 Jews were killed in the Ukraine and Belarus. Blaming the Jews for their loss of World War I, an anti-Semitic group in Germany murdered Jewish political leader Walther Rathenau.

At about that time, laws discriminating against Jews were passed in many European countries, including Latvia, Romania, and Greece. Despite the fact that approximately 40,000 Jews had served in the Austro-Hungarian army during World War I, both Austria and Hungary enacted anti-Jewish laws in the following years. Some governments even placed a limit on the percentage of Jews who could attend college. They believed limiting the Jewish people's education would prevent them from gaining too much power.

In other countries, however, Jews were treated with far more respect. One example was France, which boasted a Jewish prime minister in Leon Blum. But even in Poland, where Jews were thriving in all walks of professional life, anti-Semitism ran rampant before and after World War I.

Beer Hall Putsch

The failed attempt by the Nazis to take over the government in 1923 is known as the Beer Hall Putsch (revolt). The event earned that name because Hitler and his fellow Nazis marched in the Bürgerbräukeller Beer Hall in the city of Munich to proclaim a revolution. They then marched toward the center of town, where they were met by armed police. Gunshots rang out, and the revolt was quickly quelled.

Germany. But at that time, the Nazi Party had no power to implement policy. In 1923, the Party attempted to stage an overthrow of the government. When it failed, Hitler was sent to jail.

In jail, Hitler wrote an autobiography titled *Mein Kampf* (*My Struggle*), in which he blamed the world's ills on the Jews. He linked the Jews with communism, a political ideology he felt threatened Germany and the economic future of Europe.

Upon his release from jail, Hitler had been nearly forgotten. Germany's financial hardship had begun to disappear by the mid-1920s. Those who had been intrigued by Hitler a few years earlier were no longer attracted to the former Austrian hobo.

Hitler, though, had made a decision. He would work within the system to gain power. He would curb his violent anti-Semitism—at least in public—to earn respect from the German people. And he would bide his time until the moment was right to implement his plan. He would not have to wait long.

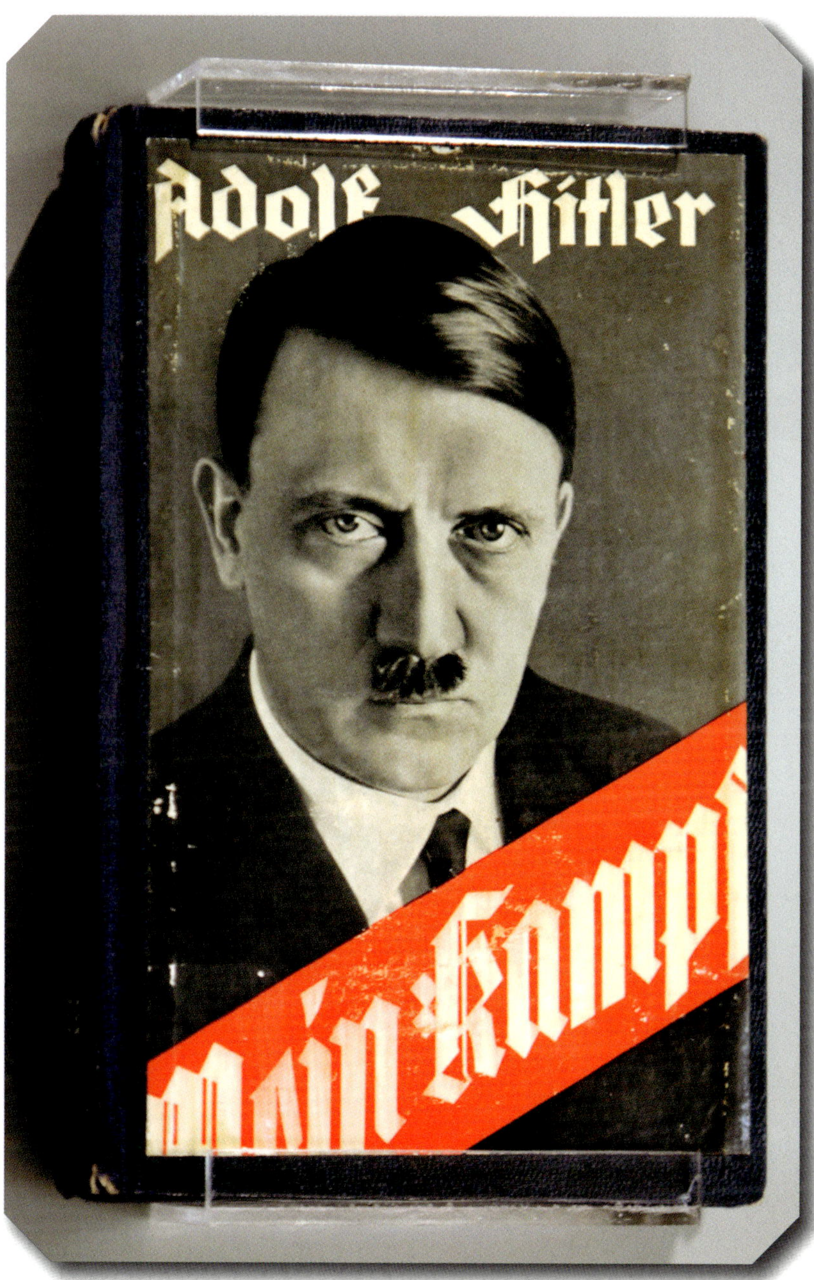

A copy of Mein Kampf, Hitler's autobiography, on display at the Holocaust Museum in Jerusalem, Israel

A group of Nazi supporters met in 1922. The party grew during the 1920s.

FANNING THE FLAMES

It has been said that if the leaders of the world had read Hitler's *Mein Kampf*, both World War II and the Holocaust could have been avoided. The book outlined his plans to destroy Jewish life in Europe and to launch a war in the East.

His stated goal was to provide *Lebensraum* (living space) for the German people.

Hitler also explained how he could sway the German masses through his speeches. He proved the theory that a big lie is more effective than a small one. He felt if he told the German people over and over again that Jews were their enemy, they would eventually believe it.

An Unstable Economy

Most Germans were not listening in the mid-1920s. They were basking in the glow of peace and a booming economy. During that time, Hitler solidified his position as Nazi Party leader and organizer. The group's numbers were growing, but not yet on a national level. In the 1928 elections, the Nazis received fewer than 3 percent of the German vote. And though anti-Semitism certainly existed, the country's 500,000 Jews remained well respected in all walks of life.

Everything changed following the stock market crash of 1929 in the United States. On October 29, panicking stockholders sold millions of shares. Prices fell, and some investors lost all their savings. The global economy collapsed. Millions of Germans lost their jobs and became destitute. Countries across the globe felt the effects of what quickly became known as the Great Depression.

Their hardship was exactly what Hitler needed to gain a mass following. He told everyone what they wanted to hear. He claimed he could make Germany great again. He claimed he could put money in their pockets. He claimed he could wipe out unemployment. And he claimed the Jews were to blame for their financial woes.

Nazi Popularity

Hitler's play upon people's anger worked. In 1930, the Nazis enjoyed a significant jump in the polls with 20 percent of the vote. That gave them 107 seats in the Reichstag, which is the German parliament. Suddenly, the Nazis were the second-most powerful party in the country. The popularity of Hitler and the Nazis continued to grow alongside the number of unemployed in Germany, which reached a staggering total of 7 million people in 1932. Though most did not embrace Hitler's ranting about the Jews, they did believe something drastic needed to be done to bring the nation out of its economic depression.

Hitler never spoke to the public about the extermination of Jews. But he did convince Germans of his belief that there was an international Jewish conspiracy to take over the world.

The "Master Race"

The Nazis firmly believed they evolved from a mystic race called Aryans, who were blond and blue-eyed. They thought the white Aryan race, as represented by the Germans, was superior to all others. Though science has debunked their theories, they considered anyone who was not

Targeting Teachers

Jews were not the only Germans who had been fired as teachers by the mid-1930s. Those who were considered "unreliable" were also banished.

Hitler wanted the Nazi ideology taught in German schools. Included in the teaching were the beliefs in the superiority of the Aryan race and the hatred of Jews. Teachers who showed hesitation to impart such Nazi beliefs to children were removed from their profession and often jailed.

a white Aryan to be inferior. Hitler, who was not blond, planned to rule Europe and use the people of eastern European countries, such as Poland, as Germany's slaves.

Such a philosophy would not have been dangerous had Hitler remained out of power. But on January 30, 1933, Germany's president, Paul von Hindenburg, named Hitler chancellor. The president was persuaded by his son and friends, as well as Hitler's promise to act lawfully. Though the Nazis did not control the Reichstag and

Book Burning in Nazi Germany

One example of how the Nazis sought to influence people occurred on the campus of the University of Berlin. It happened less than four months after Adolf Hitler assumed power in 1933.

The Nazis had deemed thousands of books to be anti-German. Many were works of tremendous literary value, including those by such famed Germans as Thomas Mann and Hugo Preuss. The books of non-German authors such as Upton Sinclair, Jack London, Helen Keller, and H. G. Wells were also banned, as were the writings of scientist Albert Einstein and psychologist Sigmund Freud.

Thousands of students screamed with joy as they lit a fire under the books. As the fire consumed the pages of the great works, German Propaganda Minister Joseph Goebbels spoke to the students. "The soul of the German people can again express itself," he said. "These flames not only illuminate the final end of an old era; they also light up the new."[1]

The book burnings were not performed solely at the University of Berlin. Similar ceremonies were taking place in colleges throughout the country.

many Germans disagreed with his views, Hitler could now work inside the government to implement his policies.

Still, Hitler was not satisfied. He deceived his cabinet members by lying to them. The Nazis used fear to give him more authority. They succeeded in burning down the Reichstag building in February 1933, and they blamed the communists. In the midst of this chaotic situation, a new legal decree signed by the president gave further power to the government. This allowed Hitler to suspend all civil liberties in the country. Within months, all other parties were banned, and the media was under Nazi control. Hitler continued to make false promises and pledged to rule peacefully. His supporters threatened violence to any who opposed him. In March 1933, Hitler's Enabling Act was approved by voters. This act established Hitler as dictator.

Awareness Overseas

Many in the United States grew alarmed at the events in Germany soon after Hitler became chancellor in 1933. Thousands of Jews in New York City organized a protest against German Nazism at Madison Square Garden on March 27. The event made millions in the United States aware of what was happening in Germany.

*Nazi troops sing in front of Woolworth Co. as a form of protest.
It was believed the company was founded by Jews.*

Planting the Seeds for the Holocaust

The Nazis wasted little time in taking steps to remove Jews from prominent positions in society. Only a small number were immediately tortured, killed, or sent to concentration camps, which had begun to spring up soon after Hitler became chancellor. But Jews were quickly banned from journalism, teaching, politics, entertainment, and other professional endeavors. Jews were banned from the German military. Hitler's private army, the *Sturmabteilung* (SA), often stood in front of Jewish-owned stores and urged Germans to boycott them. Other shops refused to serve Jewish customers.

In the summer of 1935, in the German capital of Berlin, the first organized terror campaign against the Jews began. Some Jewish-owned shops were destroyed, and Jewish citizens were beaten.

On September 15, Hitler's Nazi Party enacted the first of the Nuremberg Laws, which declared Jews to be a separate race. The Nuremberg Laws also denied German citizenship to Jews. They outlawed marriages and sexual intercourse

Too Much Power

In 1934, the Nazis destroyed the SA, their own army. The SA was a violent group that had been used to beat up political opponents and to win the support of the cautious German army during the Nazi rise to power. By the end of 1933, there were 4.5 million men in the SA. Some of the SA's leaders disagreed with Hitler. Rumors circulated that the SA was arming for a revolt. The Nazis believed the SA was becoming too powerful, so in 1934 many of its leaders were shot, and the group was disbanded. The event became known as the Blood Purge.

between Jews and other Germans. One law even forbade Jews from flying the German flag.

Many Jews decided to leave Germany at that time. Others believed the Nuremberg Laws would mark the end of the campaign against them. But they were wrong. It was only the beginning.

A crowd gathers as students throw "un-German" books into a huge fire.

Hitler, Goebbels, and other Nazi Party members watch the 1936 Olympics.

ROAD OF NO RETURN

In 1936, the persecution of German Jews was put on hold. That year, the nation was about to host the Summer Olympics, and the government sought to make a good impression on the rest of the world.

Workers busily hauled down anti-Jewish signs throughout Berlin, where the Games were to take place. It was important to put a good face on Nazism. No country boycotted the event, despite the fact that the well-publicized Nuremberg Laws were about to make Jews second-class citizens in Germany. Hitler had made certain the new laws would not take hold until after the Olympics passed.

Taking over Austria

In March 1938, Hitler and the Nazis took a step toward war by annexing Austria. The approximately 180,000 Jews of that small country were terrorized. Many people in Austria, which had been a hotbed of anti-Semitism for decades, looked on with satisfaction. They smiled and jeered as Nazis forced Jews to clean the sidewalks and gutters of Vienna. Many cheered as Jewish shops were destroyed and robbed, and their owners beaten. Some Jewish men were dragged away, and most were never seen again by their families.

The treatment of Austrian Jews was merely a precursor of the brutality to come for those in Germany. Several laws were enacted in the spring of 1938 that restricted Jews from owning a business. And in September of that year, Jewish doctors were forbidden to treat Aryan patients. Jewish lawyers were barred from their profession altogether.

On June 9, the synagogue in Munich was set on fire. Six days later, an estimated 1,500 Jews with police records—even those with minor traffic violations—were sent to concentration camps. By September, 4,000 Austrian Jews were also in concentration camps.

In late October 1938, approximately 17,000 immigrant Jews were deported to Poland. That angered 17-year-old Herschel Grynszpan, a Jewish student in Paris whose family was among those who had been shipped off. He set off to the German Embassy in Paris with the intention of killing the ambassador. Instead, a lower secretary, Ernst vom Rath, was sent out to meet Grynszpan, who shot the German official dead.

NIGHT OF THE BROKEN GLASS

The Nazis used the incident in Paris as an excuse to launch the most violent attack against the Jews to date. They claimed the uprising by the people of Germany against the Jews on the night of November 9, 1938, was spontaneous. However, the event had been planned to the last detail by Nazi leaders such as Goebbels, Hermann Goering, and SS heads Heinrich Himmler and Reinhard Heydrich.

A man brings a broom to help clean up the aftermath of Kristallnacht.

On that evening, hundreds of Jewish synagogues throughout the country were burned to the ground. Jewish shops in Germany and Austria were smashed and looted. Thousands of Jews were killed on the streets, in their homes, and in concentration camps. It would be forever known as Kristallnacht—Night of the Broken Glass—because of the shards of shattered glass that covered the streets.

Kristallnacht set Germany on a path that it would follow to the end of the war. Though the Wannsee

Conference was still a few years away, the Nazi policy from that point forward was a deadly one. The public was now involved. They could not claim to have been ignorant of the treatment of Jews. No longer were Jews simply harassed. They were arrested, occasionally tortured, or killed.

As if the brutality of Kristallnacht were not enough, the Nazis forced the Jews to pay for the damage inflicted upon them that night. Nazis claimed the Jews owed the government approximately $300 million for the murder of Rath. Additionally, the Jews were forced to hand over to the Germans any insurance money they received for their destroyed property. Finally, a new law stipulated Aryan Germans could no longer employ Jews. In other words, the vast majority of Jews could no longer work.

After these laws were passed, Jews left the country in droves. More than half of the combined 700,000 Jews in Germany and Austria had emigrated by the beginning of 1939. Unfortunately, many moved to France, Holland, and eastern

Jewish Suicides

The Nazi terror against Austrian Jews in March 1938 reached epidemic proportions. Nine Jews in the capital city of Vienna committed suicide in the two months before the Nazis annexed Austria. In the two weeks following the takeover, many more Jews in Vienna killed themselves, some even as the Nazi Gestapo was coming up the stairs to take them away.

European countries such as Poland, where they were still in danger.

By March 1939, the leaders of other countries such as England and France finally realized Hitler had lied about his peaceful intentions. Germany had marched into Czechoslovakia and was threatening Poland. Europe seemed to be on the brink of war for the second time in a little more than 20 years. World governments were still recovering from the Great Depression. Accommodating thousands of Jewish immigrants was either not a priority for such countries or was rejected as harmful to their economic health.

Then, on September 1, 1939, Germany attacked Poland. France and England declared war on Germany two days later but took a defensive stand, doing virtually nothing to help Poland. The 3.5 million Jews of that country were about to experience the full brunt of Nazi mass murder. Six Nazi death camps—Auschwitz-Birkenau, Belzec, Chelmno, Majdanek, Sobibor, and Treblinka—were eventually established in Poland. These death camps were set up specifically for killing prisoners, but other prisoners in the camps were forced into hard labor.

The six main Nazi death camps were spread throughout occupied Poland.

Hitler watches and salutes as German troops march through Warsaw in occupied Poland.

DARKNESS FALLS OVER EUROPE

The savagery used by the Nazis against German Jews paled in comparison to what was to come in Poland. The rapidity in which Germany conquered that nation was the result of a new type of warfare. Germany would eventually use the method to conquer other European nations, including Belgium, the Netherlands, France, and Greece.

Blitzkrieg

The military unveiled an aggressive and lightning-fast type of invasion called a blitzkrieg. It consisted of an overwhelming number of tanks rolling over the enemy at tremendous speeds while bomber planes attacked from the air. Poland surrendered just four weeks after the attack began.

As German troops secured the cities and villages of Poland, both the troops and SS men displayed what has been described as the most brutal treatment of fellow human beings ever witnessed. They amused themselves by kicking and beating Jews in the street. They pulled at their victims' beards and forced them at gunpoint to do the same to each other.

A Hatred of Jews

The SS elicited the help of other local citizens to join its death squads. These new members included Ukrainians, Romanians, Lithuanians, Hungarians, and the Dutch. One unknown Dutchman who served with the SS in the Soviet Union wrote a letter to a friend back in Holland. The letter was found after the war.

"This place is crawling with [Jews]," it read, "though I don't think many will be left by the time the war is over . . . I myself have shot down a whole plague of them . . . I only hope to get the chance of leading a group of comrades when we start rooting out the Jew vermin back home."[1]

Blitzkrieg warfare helped the German army invade and occupy Poland in 1939.

Just two days after the invasion of Poland was launched, an SS group entered the town of Wieruszow. Their actions there were typical of what was to follow. They herded 20 Jewish men to the market square to be executed. When a little girl ran to her father to say good-bye, an SS man ordered her to open her mouth, whereupon he placed his gun into it and pulled the trigger. The girl fell dead to the ground.

An Eyewitness to Murder

The violence continued. One Jewish boy who managed to survive the war was Arek Hersh. He described what he witnessed after the Germans had taken over his town of Sieradz.

I saw German soldiers dragging Jewish men from their houses, and kicking and beating them in the street; with horror I noticed that my father was among them. The Jewish men were forced to run towards the market place, whereupon two rows of armed German soldiers were waiting for them. They then had to run through the German gauntlet where they were savagely kicked and clubbed with rifle butts. My cousin . . . was kicked to death.[2]

Such scenes were seen throughout Poland from the first day of the war. It was common for the SS to lock up Jews in synagogues, set the buildings on fire, and shoot all who tried to escape. In the city of Bedzin, 200

Hans Frank

The Jews were not the only Poles murdered by German troops and SS men. Hitler believed all Poles were subhuman. His plan was to kill the most educated Poles and make the rest slaves for the German people.

After Poland had been conquered, Hitler appointed a German lawyer named Hans Frank as governor-general. Frank understood that his job included ordering the murder of millions of Polish people.

"If I wished to order that one should hang up posters about every seven Poles shot," Frank told a Nazi journalist, "there would not be enough forests in Poland with which to make the paper for these posters."[3]

men, women, and children were murdered in this way.

The killings received full approval from the German government and court system, although some in the army were horrified by what they were doing. On September 10, 1939, only weeks after the German invasion of Poland, a group of SS men rounded up 50 Jews, shoved them into a synagogue, and shot them all. The army brought the killers to trial, but the army judge ruled that the SS men were sickened by the sight of Jews and had acted in a spirit of adventure. They were handed mild sentences that were overturned by SS leader Heinrich Himmler. Future charges against Nazi killers were dispensed with.

Soon, hundreds of thousands of Jews, including many transported from Germany, were forced from their homes and sent into Polish ghettos in major cities such as Warsaw and Lodz. Nearly everything they owned was confiscated before they were herded onto trains headed for the ghettos.

Surrounded by barbed wire, brick walls, and armed guards, Jews—often numbering in the tens of thousands—were stuffed into cramped rooms and given little to eat. Escaping from the ghettos was nearly impossible. Thousands starved to death or died of diseases such as cholera and typhus. Others were beaten or shot by German guards for no other reason than that they were Jews.

The Nazis soon targeted Jews in the Soviet Union. In June 1941, Hitler shocked the world when he sent millions of troops into the largest country in the world. The attack took the Soviet leadership by complete surprise, and the German armies were able to march deep into enemy territory.

Hitler Targets the Soviet Union

Hitler had railed against communism for years. And in the 1930s, the Soviet Union was the only communist country in the world.

But Hitler wanted to invade Poland, and he needed to make certain the Soviet Union would not object. So he signed a nonaggression pact with the Soviet Union. It stated that Poland would be divided up between the two countries after it had been conquered by Germany. The Soviets did not realize Hitler did not plan to keep this agreement.

Germany maintained friendly relations with the Soviets as Hitler's armies overran much of Europe. But by the spring of 1941, Soviet leader Joseph Stalin was receiving intelligence messages that Germany was about to attack his country as well. He did not believe the reports. He refused to prepare his military for a possible German onslaught.

Then, on June 22 of that year, a force of more than 3 million German troops poured into the Soviet Union and met virtually no resistance. Hundreds of Soviet warplanes were bombed, and tens of thousands of prisoners were taken in the first few days.

Hitler believed the Soviet Union would be conquered almost as quickly as Poland had been. Instead, the Soviets fought back and played a major role in the defeat of Germany in World War II.

A German killing squad fires at Soviet civilians in Kiev. The civilians are sitting next to their own mass grave.

The Killing Squads

This time, however, the German armies were followed by four separate killing armies called *Einsatzgruppen* (Operational Squads). The Einsatzgruppen had been assigned the task of rounding up Jews in the cities, towns, and villages the German army had subdued. They then ordered the Jews to march up to ditches that were to serve as their own graves. The Jews were forced to undress.

They were then shot in the back of the head and tossed into the pits. The next group of Jews would meet the same fate. They were pushed atop those already in the ditch until hundreds or even thousands were dead. Some squads placed Jews who were still alive facedown in the pits and shot them in the nape of the neck.

For more than a year, the death squads continued to murder Jews. In the spring of 1942, Himmler decided this method of murder was actually taking too large an emotional toll on the shooters, and the bullets were too expensive. He ordered a new way of killing. The Jews were told they were being transported to another location, and then they were crammed into vans. Then the exhaust fumes were fed into the vehicles by hoses.

But only 20 to 25 Jews could be killed at a time by gas vans. That was

Death Squads

SS leaders took pride in their death squads and even exaggerated the number of Jews murdered to please their superiors. Adolf Eichmann bragged that the four Einsatzgruppen squads killed 2 million people, nearly all of them Jews. But studies have shown the figure was much less than 1 million.

a scale of murder far too small for Hitler, Himmler, and Heydrich. Soon extermination centers would be working at full capacity. The number of Jews being killed would soon be in the millions.

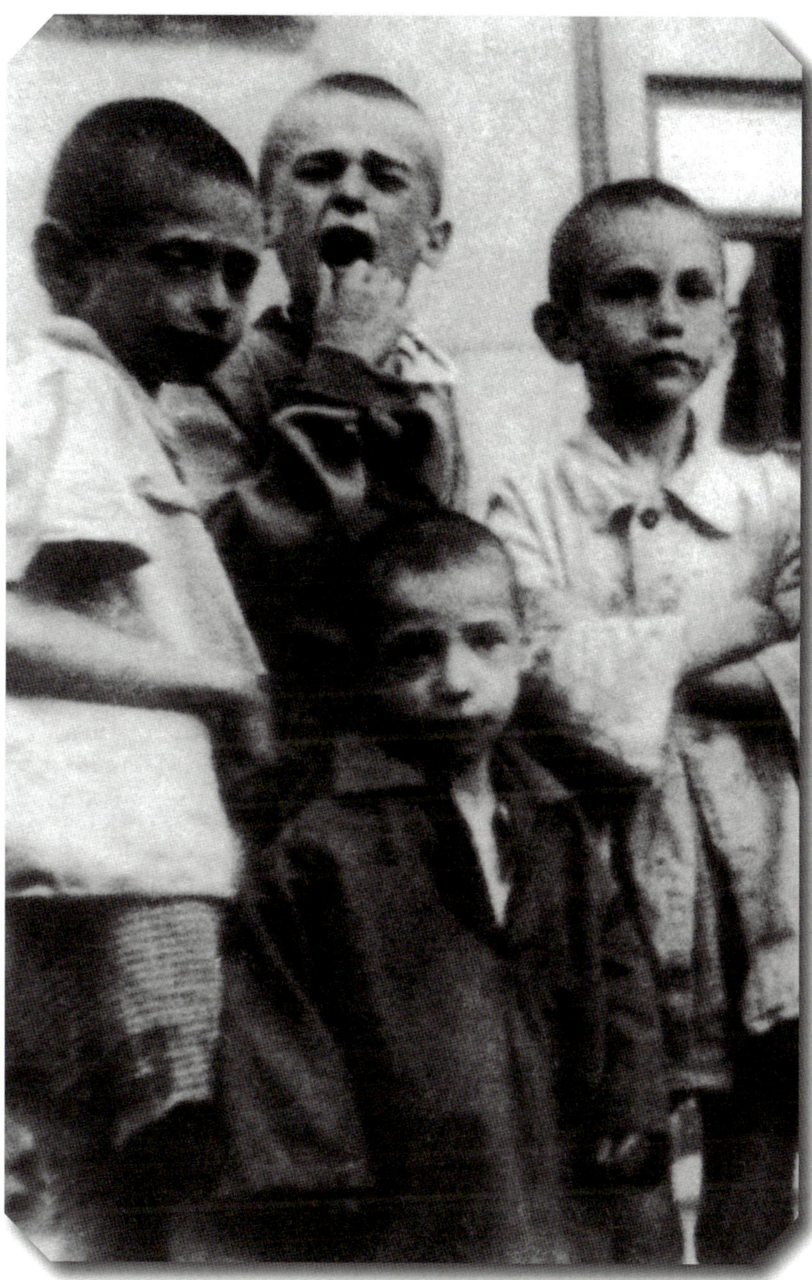

Starving children in the Warsaw ghetto in Poland

A group of Jews is taken out of the Warsaw ghetto in 1943.

From Ghettos to Gas

In May of 1940, the nations of western Europe fell quickly to Germany. Through blitzkrieg, the Germans rolled over Denmark, Norway, Belgium, and the Netherlands. The Nazis stunned the world by conquering France in a mere six weeks. Only England held out—and the Germans were bombing that country on a nightly basis.

Wherever the Nazis went, brutality followed. Mass murder requires organization, and the SS soon became masters at carrying out the methodical system that would kill as many Jews as possible in a short period of time.

While the Einsatzgruppen squads were gunning down the Jews of the Soviet Union, Jews in western Europe were receiving different treatment. In Belgium, for instance, they were kicked out of the government and from professions such as teaching, journalism, and practicing law. Soon they were banned from all management positions, and then from attending schools. They were also forced to sell their properties and wear a yellow Star of David badge in public. Jews in many countries were forced to wear

The Portrayal of Jews

Throughout their reign, the Nazis attempted to defend their treatment of the Jews by portraying them as dirty, deceiving, and inhuman. Such was the case when, following their takeover of Poland in 1940, the Germans created a propaganda documentary called *The Eternal Jew*. They used film of starving Polish Jews congregating on the streets and made wild accusations about them in an attempt to justify their treatment. The narrator described the Jews as rats while footage of crawling rats flashed across the screen. What was not mentioned was that they were ragged and starving because the Nazis had been working to drive them out.

this badge, making them easily identifiable by the German government and the public.

Fighting Back in Warsaw

By late 1942, word had come back to the Jews of the Warsaw ghetto that those who had been transported out of the ghetto had been exterminated at Treblinka, a death camp near Warsaw.

On the morning of April 19, 1943, the remaining Jews at the ghetto were determined to fight back. When a heavily armed SS unit of more than 1,000 men stormed the ghetto, the area was defended by a defiant civilian population. The Germans had 135 machine guns. The Jews had smuggled in two. The Germans had 1,358 rifles. The Jews had 15. The Germans had tanks, artillery, flame-throwers, and dynamite squads. The Jews had none.

Yet, despite it all, the resistance lasted a month. The Jews survived by using homemade grenades and showing a fierce will to live. Families hid in homemade fortified bunkers and even sewers.

In the end, however, they had no chance. On May 16, 1943, SS Brigadier General Jürgen Stroop, who was hanged for his crimes after the war, explained the final battle in his battle report. "One hundred eighty Jews, bandits and subhumans were destroyed," he wrote. "The former Jewish quarter of Warsaw is no longer in existence."[1]

In all, 7,000 Jews were killed in door-to-door fighting, and the surviving 30,000 were sent to Treblinka for execution.

Some Jews of western Europe were beaten and killed. Many men were sent to the labor camps that were springing up throughout the region. While the Germans dealt with the Jews of western Europe with less severity than they did elsewhere, all would eventually be considered targets of the Final Solution.

It had been decided at the Wannsee Conference that the Jews of the Netherlands, Belgium, and France would be transported east. They would become either slave laborers or be gassed at extermination camps. However, these plans were delayed. Many local Polish Jews had already died of starvation and disease in ghettos in places such as Warsaw, Krakow, and Lodz. The Nazis turned their attention to those who remained.

Transported to Their Deaths

The first phase of the Final Solution was deportation. Many Jews from both inside and outside the Polish ghettos were shot or beaten to death as they were rounded up. The Lublin ghetto was the first to be annihilated; others in Poland followed. The Jews of the Warsaw ghetto were either killed or sent to the nearby extermination camp named Auschwitz-Birkenau. The Jews of western Europe were also shipped to the death camps. There were six main Nazi death camps in Poland. In addition to these, there were approximately 9,000 labor camps spread throughout areas occupied by Germany.

The deportations proved as terrifying and deadly as life in the ghettos. The Jews were stuffed into

Barbed wire covers the only opening of the train car packed with prisoners being transported to a concentration camp.

cattle cars with little air, no food, and no water. Those Jews who were rounded up in France or Denmark were forced to travel for as long as a week. The majority of them died before they arrived at the camps.

The deadliest of the extermination centers was Auschwitz in Poland. Upon arrival, the victims were separated into two groups. The few deemed useful were put to work. The vast majority—women, children, the elderly, and those who were chosen randomly—were killed immediately. Often children were torn away from their parents. They would never see each other again.

Some Jews were given postcards on which they were told to write to family back home to say they were fine. That prevented loved ones, who were likely to be transported to Auschwitz, from realizing it was an extermination camp. The postcards also provided the Nazis with addresses of additional Jews.

The ones selected for immediate death noticed the sign at the entrance of the gas chambers deceptively read "Baths." As they filed in, Jewish inmate musicians played light and cheery music. The musicians had been lured into performing with the false promise of having their lives spared in exchange.

Auschwitz

It has been estimated that more than 1 million Jews were murdered at the Auschwitz camp alone. Today, Auschwitz exists as a historical museum to tell the stories of the Jews who died there and as proof that the Holocaust did indeed happen.

Auschwitz Prisoner Identification

Nazi guards who worked at Auschwitz dehumanized their prisoners. Upon arrival, those who were deemed strong enough to work were stripped of their possessions. Their heads were shaved and they were each tattooed with an identification number. The prisoners were no longer referred to by their names.

These marks ensured the prisoner could be identified after death. The guards had experimented with sewing the identification numbers onto the prisoners' clothes, but when a prisoner died and was stripped, there was no way to identify him. Early in the war, the tattoo was placed on a prisoner's left breast. Later, it was moved to the inner forearm. After the war, these tattoos became the distinguishing mark of an Auschwitz survivor.

SHOWERS WITHOUT DRAINS

Some of the gas chambers could hold up to 2,000 victims. Just outside, the Jews were told to undress because they were going to take a shower. They were even given towels. But once inside, they undoubtedly realized something was horribly wrong—there were no drains. The huge door was locked behind them. Above them were vents, into which crystals of hydrogen cyanide called Zyklon-B were poured.

The executioners would watch the scene from a porthole. The roomful of victims, often clinging families, remained stunned until they grasped the horror of the events. Some prayed, others panicked. They would claw at each other and themselves.

About a half hour later, the screams of terror would end. Pumps blew away the poisonous air. Another group of Jews would drag the bodies out. In exchange, these Jews had been promised their lives and enough food to prevent starvation.

After the war, the German public claimed they knew nothing about what was happening to the Jews. But there is no doubt that others, outside those planning and participating in the transportation and murder of the victims, were quite aware of the Jews' plight. German businessmen battled for contract bids to provide necessities in the extermination process, such as poison gas and the furnaces to cremate the bodies.

A company called I. A. Topf & Sons of Erfurt was granted the contract to produce the crematoria at Auschwitz. A letter from the firm to the SS representatives at the camp stated, "We acknowledge receipt of your order for five triple furnaces, including two electric elevators for raising the corpses and one emergency elevator. A practical installation for stoking coal was also ordered and one for transporting ashes."[2]

SS Control

Filip Müller was one Jew who was promised his life at Auschwitz if he helped drag the victims from the gas chambers. He was wracked with guilt that his life had been spared while other Jews were being sent to die.

On one occasion, he ran into the gas chamber to commit suicide. He felt a sense of calm rush over him, but he was pushed out the door. He was then beaten by an SS man named Kurschuss.

"You bloody [idiot]," Kurschuss yelled at Müller, "get it into your stupid head: *we* decide how long you stay alive and when you die, and not you."[3]

The cold disregard for human life was perhaps most noticeable at the extermination camps, where the mass murder of Jews was done in the name of racial purity. For one group of Nazis, though, torture and killing were performed for what they claimed to be the advancement of medical science.

The charred remains found in the crematorium at
Buchenwald concentration camp

SS leader Himmler faces a prisoner at a camp in the Soviet Union. He authorized medical experimentation on the prisoners.

Guinea Pigs and Revenge

From 1942 to 1945, hundreds of thousands of Jews and non-Jews were in the concentration camps. At the urging of SS leader Heinrich Himmler, approximately 200 medical doctors took advantage of this opportunity to conduct ghastly experiments on Jews and other prisoners.

The medical "research" on concentration camp inmates included placing them in high altitude chambers until they stopped breathing. Others were given lethal injections of typhus and jaundice or forced to lie naked in the snow until they froze to death. New weapons were tried on them. Some were shot with poison bullets or exposed to mustard gas.

Among the supposed medical professionals participating in the experiments was Professor August Hirt of the Reich University of Strasbourg in France. Hirt wrote SS Lieutenant General Rudolf Brandt of his plans. First, experiments would be conducted on a large group of Jewish prisoners of war from the Soviet Union. They would then be gassed to death and sent to him. Hirt would cut off their skulls and begin his research. "By procuring the skulls of [Russian Jews], who represent the prototype of the repulsive, but characteristic, subhuman," he wrote, "we have the chance now to obtain scientific material."[1]

Further Exploitation

The Jews were exploited by the Nazis even after their deaths. Following their executions in the gas chambers, victims were searched for gold teeth. The teeth were extracted, melted down, and banked for the war effort.

Hirt planned on detecting differences in the corpses to prove the inferiority of the Jewish race. The research would be saved for posterity because he believed Jews were in the process of becoming extinct.

Perhaps the most notorious doctor conducting research was Josef Mengele, whose experiments were in line with advancing Nazi racial policy. He carried out tests on twins gathered from occupied Europe in an attempt to discover a way for German women to bear more than one child at a time. The goal was to develop a race of super Aryans.

The White Rose Letters

Not all Germans agreed with the extreme policies and actions of the Nazi regime. Some risked their lives to protest. Among them was a group of University of Munich students led by a brave young woman named Sophie Scholl. Along with her brother Hans and a philosophy professor named Kurt Huber, Scholl had become disgusted with the Nazi treatment of Jews. She also foresaw disaster in the Soviet Union, where Germany was losing the war.

The Scholls, Huber, and others began secretly distributing anti-Nazi literature that became known as the "White Rose Letters." The protestors understood that if they were discovered, it would mean certain death.

In early 1943, a building superintendent at the university saw Scholl tossing leaflets from a balcony. He turned her over to authorities.

Nazi courts were not in place to give fair trials. Their purpose was to punish anyone who worked against the regime. But Scholl stood up to the verbal attacks of Nazi judge Roland Freisler, asking him why he was too cowardly to admit the war was lost. But it was no use. Huber, the Scholls, and several other students were executed by beheading.

Mengele and other German physicians tortured both children and adults. They placed various chemicals in the eyes of their victims to study their reactions. The physicians would then kill them by injecting chloroform into their hearts. Afterward, the physicians would examine their internal organs.

Mengele and Hirt both conducted other deadly research, as did other Nazi doctors. It was estimated that 7,000 men, women, and children were subjected to these cruel experiments. The vast majority did not survive.

Josef Mengele's Death

Josef Mengele escaped justice following the war. The man who conducted hideous experiments on prisoners at Auschwitz disappeared in 1945. He continued to hide from the law in South America. In 1985, he was finally identified as the victim of a simple drowning accident that had occurred in Brazil six years earlier.

REVENGE

Meanwhile, SS troops were massacring thousands of innocent people in various parts of Europe. One notorious incident occurred in the small village of Lidice in Czechoslovakia. On May 29, 1942, two Czech resistance fighters had killed SS leader Reinhard Heydrich by tossing a bomb into his car. The Nazis immediately executed more than 1,000 Czechs, but it was the Jews who suffered the most. Three thousand were removed from the ghetto of

In addition to hard labor and starvation, prisoners were subjected to torturous medical experiments.

Theresienstadt and shipped east for extermination. On the morning of June 9, 1942, hundreds of German SS troops arrived in peaceful Lidice, the hometown of the Czech assassins, and surrounded it. One boy tried to run away and was shot to death. A peasant woman who attempted to do the same was also murdered. The SS then locked every male in a barn.

The following morning, they shot all of them, ten at a time, killing some 172 innocent inhabitants.

The women and most of the children of Lidice were imprisoned or shot. Seven children deemed Aryan enough were sent off to be raised by German parents in the name of racial purity. The SS then blew up everything in Lidice and leveled off the land. The village simply ceased to exist. The destruction of the village was not an isolated incident.

The Jews of Hungary were also targeted. Hungary's fascist government had reluctantly joined the war in July 1941. Its leaders believed the country would be spared Hitler's aggression if it joined the Nazis in fighting the Soviet Union—and they were right for a while. The Germans stayed out of Hungary, although the country's 800,000 Jews were already being tormented and murdered by the anti-Semitic ruling party named the Arrow Cross.

But in 1944, the Hungarian front was collapsing, and the Soviets were advancing toward Germany. That motivated the Nazis to take over Hungary for strategic reasons. They placed hundreds of thousands of Jews into ghettos and then began

Justice for Murderers

The German commander who led the mass slaughter in Lidice was punished for his crime. Max Rostock was in charge of the operation. In 1951, he was put on trial and then hanged in the Czech capital of Prague.

transporting them to death camps in Poland. In the summer of 1944, approximately 400,000 of Hungary's 725,000 Jews were deported to Auschwitz, crammed into an average of 20 trainloads per night.

World War II was nearly over. The Soviets were fighting their way to the German capital of Berlin. The Americans had landed in France on D-day, June 6, 1944, joining the British and others in freeing the French from German rule. Now the Americans were battling their way onto German soil as well. Hitler was holed up in his bunker in Berlin. His dream of world domination was destroyed.

On their way to Berlin, both the Soviet and U.S. armies stumbled upon extermination and concentration camps such as Auschwitz, Treblinka, Dachau, and Buchenwald. It was an experience they would never forget.

Revolt against Hitler

Following D-day in June 1944, and the Soviet breakout from the east, a group of German military men decided it was time to kill Hitler and make a separate deal with the Western Allies. On July 20, 1944, an explosive hidden in a briefcase was planted at a meeting Hitler was attending. The plan was to kill Hitler, remove all the Nazis from government, and end the war. It all came crashing down, though, because Hitler survived the explosion. He then exacted revenge on anyone who was believed to have had a part in the plot. Thousands were hanged or shot. It was the last attempt on Hitler's life.

U.S. soldiers arrive to liberate Dachau.

When Allied forces arrived at Auschwitz, they found evidence of the prisoners who had suffered there, including thousands of pairs of shoes.

THE SHOCKING DISCOVERIES

Hitler once declared that the Nazi empire he created would last 1,000 years. By the middle of 1944, it became clear that it would be lucky to survive 12 more months. The Allied forces continued to advance against Germany.

The Soviets were storming their way into Poland. The Allies in the west, led by the British and Americans, had gained a foothold in France. They were beginning to push the once-invincible German armies back to their homeland.

DEATH MARCHES

The threat of almost certain defeat did not motivate the Nazis to free the Jews. Rather, they stepped up their murderous rampage against them while attempting to hide the evidence, though not always successfully.

The first step was to evacuate the slave labor camps as the Soviet troops closed in. Tens of thousands of Jews working at Auschwitz were sent to camps in Germany. They traveled on foot, embarking on brutal treks that came to be known as death marches. Others were packed tightly into trains.

Allied Strategies

During the war, as the evidence of the Holocaust mounted, it was suggested to Allied leaders that the railroad lines and the extermination camps be bombed. Bombing the railway lines could prevent the Germans from transporting people to the death camps.

The plea was rejected by U.S. President Franklin D. Roosevelt. It was decided that the best way to end the killing was to defeat Germany as quickly as possible. It has been argued, however, that destroying the railways and camps could have saved more than 1 million lives.

Prisoners too weak to survive a forced march were shot and killed immediately. Anyone who collapsed or attempted to rest during the march was also shot. The bodies were simply tossed into ditches. A group of Jews who had been evacuated by train attempted to escape near the Polish town of Leszczysy. They were murdered as they ran through the forests.

The Soviets found few prisoners when they arrived at Auschwitz on January 27, 1945. But they did discover haunting evidence of the more than 1 million exterminations performed there: 836,255 women's dresses, 348,000 men's suits, and 38,000 pairs of shoes.

GREETING IN GERMANY

Meanwhile, the death marches continued. When those who had survived reached Germany, they were often harassed by the German public. They felt the hatred of many of its people. Among these prisoners was Abraham Herman, whose daughter Marilyn recalled what he had told her about his experience.

When the prisoners were marched through German areas, women and children would smash bottles at their feet so that these prisoners, whose footwear consisted, at most, of rags tied around their feet, would rip their feet on the broken glass. By contrast, while walking through Czech territory, Czech people were throwing bread to the prisoners, and my father remembered that a woman risked her life to run out and hand him a piece of bread, ensuring that he got his piece of bread amidst the scramble, and she was hit on her head by a guard with the butt of a machine gun for her troubles.[1]

Those kept alive were saved for a purpose. They were used as slave laborers in Germany, whose leaders

Guards at Dachau

Some Nazi guards at Dachau did not escape before the U.S. soldiers arrived. Many donned prisoner uniforms in an attempt to fool the U.S. troops into believing they were victims. But their healthy bodies gave them away. At Dachau, more than 100 Nazis were beaten and killed by prisoners strong enough to take on the task. Others were shot to death by U.S. soldiers overcome by anger.

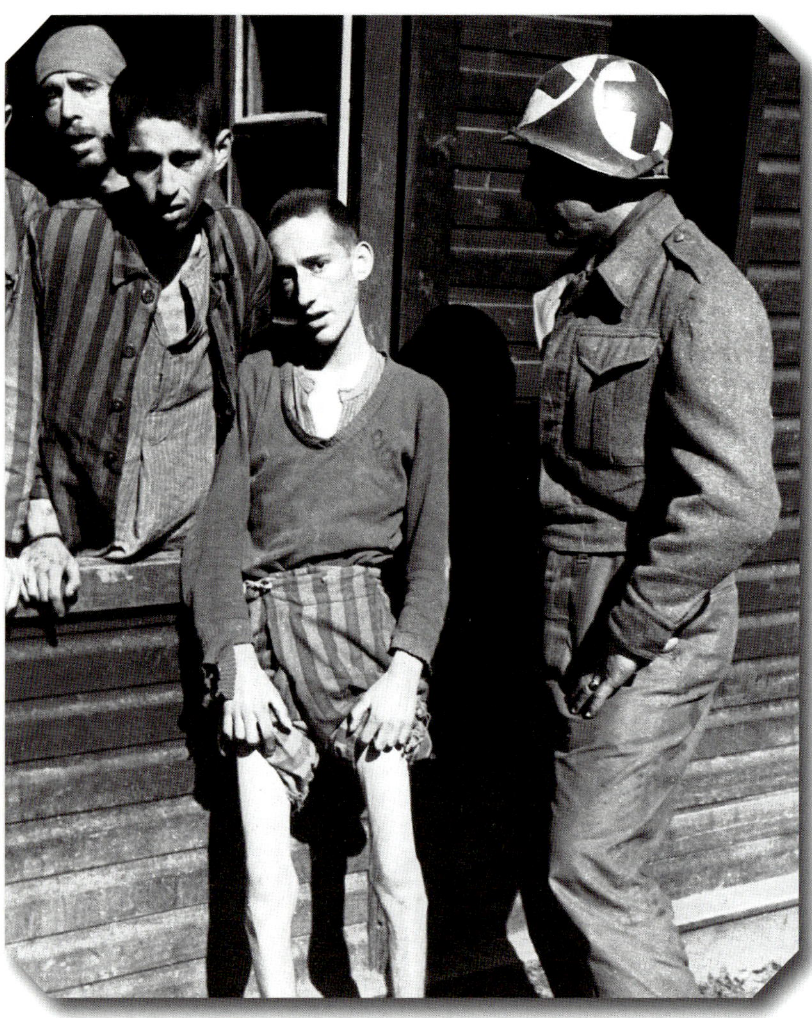

Extremely malnourished prisoners were found when U.S. troops liberated the concentration camps.

were desperate to hold off the Soviet, American, and British advances. These slave laborers were used to work in factories making weapons.

LIBERATING THE CAMPS

By early 1945, the Americans had reached German soil. On April 4, one unit stumbled upon a forced labor camp in the village of Ohrdruf. Four thousand Jews and others had been murdered there in the previous three months. Hundreds had been shot just before the liberators had arrived.

The Americans were appalled by what they saw, but they had not seen everything yet. Allied troops reached dozens of other camps on the way to Berlin. Each was populated by prisoners who looked like skeletons. The Jews of Buchenwald had been evacuated just before the Americans arrived, but the piled-up corpses and other evidence of mass murder left many liberators in tears. Army Private Harry J. Herder Jr. wrote:

> *The bodies of human beings were stacked like cord wood. . . . Human bodies neatly stacked, naked, ready for disposal. The arms and legs were neatly arranged, but an occasional limb dangled oddly. . . . There was an aisle, then another stack, and another aisle, and more stacks. The Lord only knows how many there were.*[2]

Confronting the Destruction

U.S. General George S. Patton ordered that the citizens of nearby Weimar be forced to witness what their Nazi government had perpetrated. More than 1,000 local Germans were escorted more than five miles (8 km) on foot to the Buchenwald camp. Many stood in silence. Others wept. Most claimed they never knew about the massacres there. That assertion has been debated for generations. Some believe they had to know—the stench of dead bodies could be smelled for miles.

Many of those who had survived Buchenwald were in no condition to even understand that they had been liberated. One who did was 17-year-old Benjamin Bender, who could not bring himself to be happy that he was not one of the 3 million Polish Jews to perish in the Holocaust.

> *I stood up, feeling weak. I stared at the beds around me. Motionless people, wax masks, totally unaware that finally they were free. I wanted to scream, to share with them the moment of joy, but I couldn't. There was no joy in my heart, but a gaping emptiness. . . . Wounds never turned to scars. A tormented soul had never a chance to recover. A day in Buchenwald was a lifetime in Hell.[3]*

The soldiers were braced for whatever they saw after that. Two and a half weeks later, U.S. troops entered the Dachau concentration camp. An estimated 33,000 survivors, many barely alive, were the lucky ones. The corpses were everywhere, including on the road south out of Dachau, where hundreds had been killed during a forced march.

For several years after the end of the war, tens of thousands of sick, emaciated, and homeless refugees traveled through Europe in search of a safe home.

The Story of Anne Frank

On June 12, 1942, a 13-year-old girl named Anne Frank received a diary for her birthday. Anne's life was far from ordinary, though. She was a thoughtful child who was hiding from the Nazis.

The Frank family had fled Germany to live in the Dutch city of Amsterdam after Hitler took power in 1933. When the Nazis overran Holland in 1940, the Franks and three friends moved into a secret annex.

Anne wrote in her diary daily. She expressed her fears about the persecution of Dutch Jews by the Nazis. She also wrote about personal issues such as love and relationships.

But Anne did not survive the war. On August 4, 1944, German and Dutch security police arrested the group. She was sent to the Bergen-Belsen concentration camp, where she died of typhus and starvation at age 15. The only family member to survive was her father, Otto Frank.

The day after the secret annex had been raided, pages of Anne's diary were discovered on the floor. They were later given to Otto, who eventually had them published in 1947. The book, *Anne Frank: Diary of a Young Girl,* became an immediate bestseller. It was later made into a movie. Anne Frank is one of the most symbolic of the Jewish victims of the Holocaust.

The Holocaust had taken 6 million Jewish lives from across Europe. World War II had claimed between 48 million and 79 million people. Could justice truly be served? Inside a courtroom in the Germany city of Nuremberg, an epic trial of those responsible was about to begin.

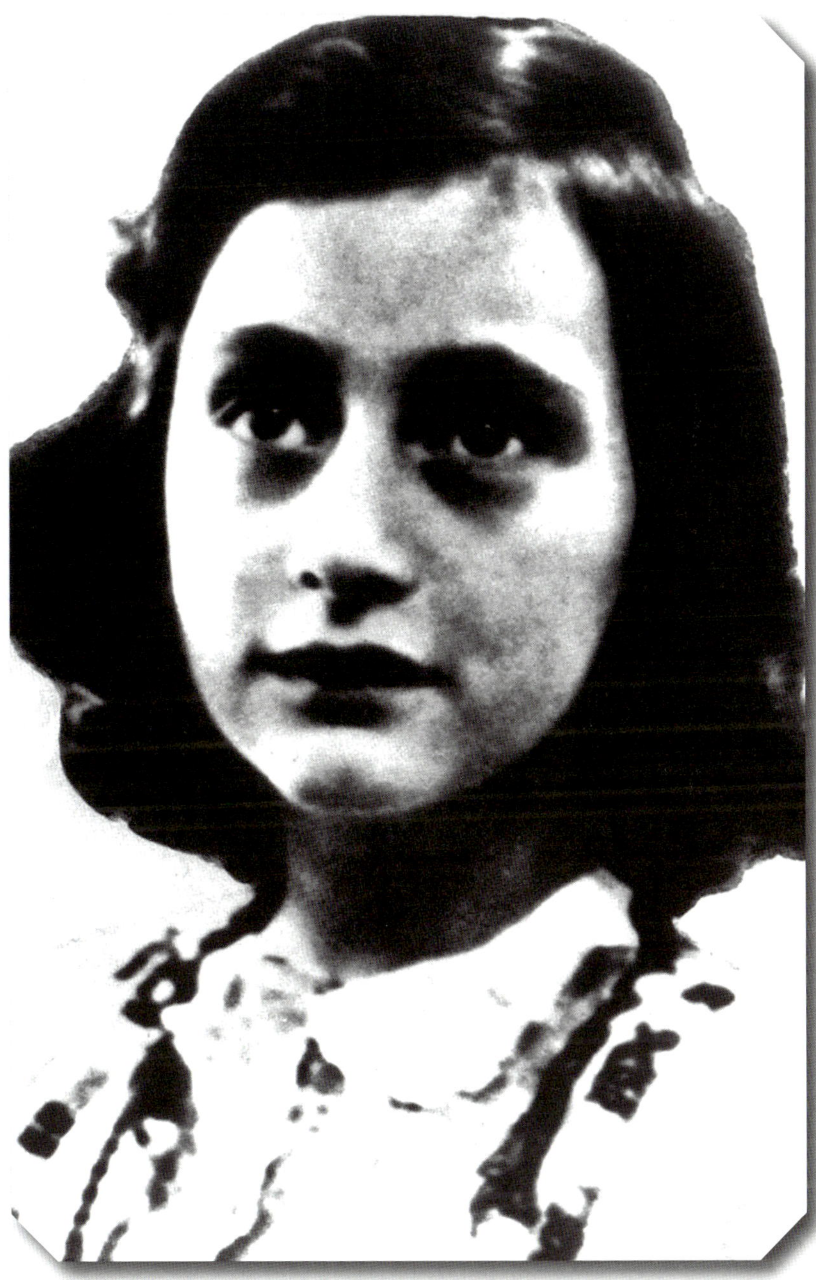

A portrait of Anne Frank

Hitler at the height of his power

JUDGMENT AT NUREMBERG

On April 30, 1945, a distraught Hitler retired to his room, stuck a revolver in his mouth, and pulled the trigger. The day before, he had married Eva Braun, who had been his mistress since the 1930s. The two committed suicide together. By provoking World War II, Hitler had caused the deaths of 50 million people. Now he added his own name to the list.

The Soviet army was destroying Berlin. The Germans were close to losing the war, and Nazi leaders realized they would not survive justice when it was meted out. Germany surrendered seven days after Hitler killed himself.

Propaganda chief Joseph Goebbels poisoned his six children and then had a Nazi attendant shoot him and his wife. SS head Heinrich Himmler donned a private's uniform and attempted to escape. When he was caught by the British, he bit down on a cyanide capsule and committed suicide.

There was plenty of blame to go around. Thousands of people had participated, not only in the planning and running of the war, but in the massacre of 6 million Jews. Trials were arranged to punish the guilty.

Following Orders

A common excuse of those who had participated in the Holocaust was that they had simply followed orders. Among those who used that excuse was Josef Kramer, who ran the Bergen-Belsen extermination camp at the end of the war. For his brutality, he earned the nickname "The Beast of Belsen."

"I had no feelings in carrying out these things, because I received an order," he told a British military tribunal. "That, incidentally, is the way I was trained."[1]

But Kramer's excuse was deemed unacceptable. Kramer was sentenced to death and executed in November 1945.

The most famous trial was held in Nuremberg starting in October 1945. It lasted just under one year. Hundreds of witnesses testified, and a film compiled during the final months of the war was screened. It showed footage of more than a dozen slave labor, concentration, and extermination camps liberated by U.S. troops. The Nazi defendants were forced to witness the horrors of decisions they had made while safely sitting behind their desks. These images included stacks of corpses, devices of torture, and emaciated bodies.

Some Nazis such as Albert Speer and Hans Frank were

suddenly repentant. Frank, the governor-general of occupied Poland stated, "A thousand years will pass and the guilt of Germany will not be erased."[2]

CRIMES AGAINST HUMANITY

Twenty-one Nazi leaders were charged with four major crimes, but those involving the Holocaust fell under the category of "Crimes against Humanity." Twelve were sentenced to death by hanging, including Frank, Armed Forces Chief of Staff Wilhelm Keitel, and Julius Streicher, editor of the anti-Semitic newspaper, *Der Stürmer*.

Though Streicher claimed he had had no direct involvement in sending Jews to their deaths, it was ruled that he had helped inspire the Holocaust. In one article, he had expressed a desire to have the Jews of the Soviet Union exterminated. In another, he claimed the father of the Jewish people was the devil and extermination was the only solution. He died on the gallows, still brimming with defiance.

Nazi Hunter

The foremost Nazi hunter since the end of World War II is a Holocaust survivor named Simon Wiesenthal. Wiesenthal, who was barely alive when he was liberated from the Mauthausen camp, went to work after the Nuremberg trials to find anyone who had played a role in the murder of the 6 million Jews. Among the hundreds he brought to justice was Adolf Eichmann, a German official responsible for the deportation of many Jews.

Defendants in the Nuremberg War Crimes Trial hear the verdict.

Hermann Goering was second-in-command to Hitler during most of the war. He was in charge of the German air force, which killed hundreds of thousands and terrorized millions. He also directed actions that resulted in the mass murder of the Jews. When he was sentenced to death by hanging, he followed Himmler's lead by taking poison and killing himself the night before he was scheduled to be hanged.

Other Trials

The Nuremberg trials were easily the most storied of all the postwar tribunals, but many others brought justice to the perpetrators of the Holocaust. Twelve trials involving 185 defendants were held in Nuremberg between 1946 and 1949. Those forced to take the stand included doctors responsible for the gruesome medical experiments, businessmen who used slave labor and created the furnaces for burning corpses, and SS men who ran the extermination camps or commanded mobile death squads. In many cases, they were put to death. Trials continued into the 1990s.

Among those put on trial were commanders and guards at death camps Majdanek, Auschwitz, Treblinka, and Sobibor. Germany has been applauded by many for owning up to its Nazi past and seeking justice for those who participated in the Holocaust.

Meanwhile, thousands of war crimes trials were also taking place in countries such as Poland, the

Aiding a Suicide

It has been claimed that a U.S. guard at Nuremberg named Tex Wheelis was responsible for providing defendant Hermann Goering with the cyanide pill that allowed him to commit suicide rather than be hanged. Wheelis had befriended Goering during the trial. Goering had given Wheelis presents, such as a gold pen and a watch. Some speculate these gifts were bribes and that Wheelis smuggled the cyanide capsule to Goering to allow him to avoid the dishonor of hanging.

Soviet Union, England, France, Hungary, Norway, and the Netherlands. The busiest court system was in Poland, where more than 5,000 suspected war criminals were tried, including guards at extermination camps Auschwitz, Majdanek, and Stutthof. Among those executed in Poland was Jürgen Stroop, who had commanded the SS troops that had brutally crushed the Warsaw Ghetto Uprising in April 1943.

Yet, many doubt the justice served after the Holocaust was enough. The job of trying and convicting everyone who participated in the Holocaust was deemed impossible. Many who killed tens, hundreds, and even thousands of Jews returned to their old careers in Germany and did get away with murder.

Adolf Eichmann is found guilty and sentenced to death.

Elie Wiesel accepts his Nobel Peace Prize.

THE HOLOCAUST IN HISTORY

Following World War II, the UN convened to discuss and rule on what had happened in Germany and throughout Europe during Hitler's reign. In 1948, the UN adopted the Convention on the Prevention and Punishment of the Crime of Genocide. The group intended to define what constitutes genocide: the intentional mass killing or harm of a large group of people, such as a religious or ethnic group. The UN also ruled that acts of genocide are crimes under international law. These are standards and principles that countries are expected to follow. The goal of the convention was to prevent acts of genocide from taking place in the future. However, even with this convention in place, genocide has occurred on smaller scales after World War II in countries such as Cambodia, Rwanda, and Bosnia. With no international police force, international laws are difficult to enforce.

TELLING THEIR STORIES

Keeping the memory of the Holocaust alive has been the goal of many people and organizations over the years. Among them is Elie Wiesel, a Romanian Jew who was a famous survivor of the Buchenwald extermination camp. Wiesel barely lived through a death march to that site from Auschwitz.

Wiesel went on to become an author, professor, poet, and political activist. He wrote eloquently about the Holocaust, advised presidents, and won a Nobel Peace Prize in 1986 for his work toward peace and human rights. Another survivor, Simon Wiesenthal, established a world-famous organization, located in Vienna, Austria, and Los Angeles, to hunt down Nazis.

In the mid-1990s, the world witnessed the war between Serbians and Croatians that resulted in mass murders justified as "ethnic cleansing." In response, Wiesel invoked the memory of the Holocaust. He made an eloquent appeal on the fiftieth anniversary of the liberation of Auschwitz.

The "Never Forget" Shrine

The desire to honor and remember the millions who died motivated the creation of the United States Holocaust Memorial Museum. It opened in Washington DC in 1993. Though other Holocaust sites exist in various U.S. cities, the one in Washington DC is considered the national memorial.

The U.S. Holocaust Memorial Museum does not spotlight solely the 6 million Jews murdered. It also honors other groups of people whom the Nazis deemed unworthy of life. Included were Gypsies, the handicapped, Poles, homosexuals, Jehovah's Witnesses, and perceived political enemies.

One permanent exhibit is simply called The Holocaust. It is divided into three parts: Nazi Assault, Final Solution, and Last Chapter. A narrative that takes visitors through the exhibit begins with images U.S. soldiers witnessed as they liberated Nazi death camps in 1945. A railcar used to transport Jews from their homes, or from the ghettos to the extermination camps, is also featured.

The Holocaust museum with the largest archive of information is called the "Yad Vashem" and is located in the Israeli city of Jerusalem. Established in 1953, the organization is committed to commemorating, documenting, researching, and educating people about the Holocaust.

As we reflect upon the past, we must address ourselves to the present and the future. In the name of all that is sacred in memory, let us stop the bloodshed in Bosnia, Rwanda, and [Chechnya]; the vicious and ruthless terror attacks against Jews in the Holy Land. Let us reject and oppose more effectively religious fanaticism and racial hate.[1]

A Famous Holocaust Denier

Iran President Mahmoud Ahmadinejad has been a visible and ardent Holocaust denier. Ahmadinejad is not alone in claiming the Holocaust never occurred. Anti-Semites and those with a hatred for Israel have made the same argument, despite overwhelming documentation. They admit the Nazis hated the Jews, but they claim the films, books, and testimony from Holocaust survivors, and even executioners, were fabricated.

Life after Liberation

Of the estimated 200,000 Jews liberated from concentration camps, about 150,000 returned to their homelands. But some were not greeted with open arms, and others discovered their houses had been destroyed during the war. Survivors who returned to Poland were sometimes threatened or even killed by their anti-Semitic neighbors.

Most could not feel joy for having survived. After all, many of their family and friends had been murdered, and the towns to which they returned were in shambles. "Who will release us from the pain in our hearts, from the lonesomeness and destruction that call out at us from every street corner and every clod of earth?" asked one displaced Jew.[2]

Iran President Mahmoud Ahmadinejad

It is quite likely that there will always be some angry people who claim the mass murder of Jews never happened. Most people believe it is important to keep the memory of the event alive so the same claim is not made by others, especially those in positions of power, such as Ahmadinejad.

That is where the mass media has played the most significant role. Several movies have served as a reminder of the horrors of the Holocaust. Among them was *Judgment at Nuremberg* (1961), which depicted a trial of Nazi judges who played a role in sending Jews and others to their deaths. A television miniseries titled *The Holocaust* (1978) sparked discussions about the subject as well. Another was *Schindler's List* (1993). Filmed in black-and-white, the movie focused on a real-life German businessman who saved the lives of hundreds of Jews at the end of the war.

In addition, the words, deeds, and writings of those dead or alive who experienced the Holocaust—not just the survivors, but the perpetrators as well—have been preserved.

Compensation for Holocaust Survivors

For those who survived the Holocaust, no amount of compensation can ever right the wrongs that were done to them. However, some Holocaust survivors and their heirs have petitioned the German government for compensation for their stolen property.

As of 2007, there were more than 75,000 unresolved claims by Jewish families for property lost or stolen. However, it is estimated that the German government has paid more than $100 billion, adjusted for inflation, in compensation to the many Holocaust victims.

Though the majority of those involved as victims and murderers are now dead, the words describing their experiences during the Holocaust serve as a testament to what happened in Europe under Adolf Hitler's reign.

A 2006 ceremony honored the sixty-first anniversary of the liberation of the Auschwitz-Birkenau concentration camp in Poland.

TIMELINE

1933

Adolf Hitler is appointed chancellor of Germany on January 30.

1933

In March, Hitler's Enabling Act is approved by voters. This act establishes Hitler as dictator.

1933

Nazis call for a boycott of Jewish shops and businesses on April 1.

1939

Hitler promotes the extermination of the Jews during a speech on January 30.

1939

The brutal treatment of Polish Jews begins as the Germans invade Poland on September 1, launching World War II.

1939

SS leader Reinhard Heydrich directs special action squads to force Polish Jews into ghettos on September 21.

1935	**1938**	**1938**
Nuremberg Laws are signed into law on September 15.	The SS begins mistreatment and murder of Jews in Austria in March.	German Jews are terrorized, taken to concentration camps, and killed on Kristallnacht on November 9.

1941	**1941**	**1942**
The Einsatzgruppen death squads follow the German army into conquered areas of the Soviet Union in July and begin the mass murder of Jews.	Nazi second-in-command Hermann Goering instructs Heydrich to prepare for the "Final Solution" on July 31.	The Wannsee Conference is held to coordinate the "Final Solution" on January 20.

TIMELINE

1942

The SS destroys the Czechoslovakian village of Lidice, the hometown of Heydrich's assassins, on June 10.

1942

The Treblinka death camp opens in Poland on July 23. Jews from the Warsaw ghetto begin arriving to be exterminated.

1943

The SS puts down Jewish resistance in the Warsaw ghetto beginning on April 19.

1945

Hitler commits suicide in his Berlin bunker on April 30. Germany surrenders seven days later.

1946

Many leading Nazis are condemned to death by hanging on October 17, following the Nuremberg trials.

1946

The trial of 23 former SS doctors and scientists who performed experiments on Jews and others begins on December 9.

1944

Jews from Hungary begin to be deported. More than 400,000 people are eventually deported.

1945

On January 27, the Soviets liberate Auschwitz, where more than 1 million Jews have been murdered.

1945

American troops liberate German death camps Buchenwald and Dachau in April.

1947

A trial of 21 Einsatzgruppen leaders begins on September 15. Fourteen are sentenced to death.

1953

Yad Vashem, a Holocaust museum, is established in Jerusalem to commemorate and document the Holocaust.

1993

The United States Holocaust Memorial Museum opens in Washington DC.

Essential Facts

Date of Event

January 30, 1933, to October 17, 1946

Place of Event

Germany, Poland, Soviet Union

Key Players

- German dictator Adolf Hitler
- SS leader Heinrich Himmler
- SS leader Reinhard Heydrich
- Coordinator of Jewish evacuation to death camps, Adolf Eichmann
- Governor-General of occupied Poland, Hans Frank

Highlights of Event

❖ The Nuremberg Laws were signed and Jewish stores were boycotted in Germany.

❖ Kristallnacht was a night of public violence and murder against Jews in Germany and Austria.

❖ The annexation of Austria and Czechoslovakia, and the conquest of Poland and areas of the Soviet Union, began the brutal treatment of Jews in foreign lands.

❖ Jews in Poland and the Soviet Union were herded into ghettos, where they were killed off or transported to concentration camps.

❖ Extermination camps were built in Poland and Germany to implement the "Final Solution"—the plan to murder all the Jews of Europe.

❖ Soviet, U.S., and British troops uncovered the horrors of the extermination camps as they marched into Germany and Poland in the final push to victory in World War II.

❖ Hundreds of leading Nazis in government and other professions were tried and executed or jailed after the war.

Quote

"As we reflect upon the past, we must address ourselves to the present and the future. In the name of all that is sacred in memory, let us stop the bloodshed in Bosnia, Rwanda, and [Chechnya]; the vicious and ruthless terror attacks against Jews in the Holy Land. Let us reject and oppose more effectively religious fanaticism and racial hate."—*Elie Wiesel, a Holocaust survivor*

ADDITIONAL RESOURCES

SELECTED BIBLIOGRAPHY

Bauer, Yehuda. *A History of the Holocaust*. New York: Franklin Watts, 2001.

Friedländer, Saul. *Nazi Germany and the Jews: The Years of Extermination*. New York: HarperCollins Publishers, 2007.

Gilbert, Martin. *Never Again: A History of the Holocaust*. New York: Universe Publishing, 2000.

Laqueur, Walter. *The Holocaust Encyclopedia*. New Haven, CT: Yale University Press, 2001.

Shirer, William L. *The Rise and Fall of the Third Reich: A History of Nazi Germany*. New York: Simon and Schuster, 1960.

FURTHER READING

Frank, Anne. *Anne Frank: The Diary of a Young Girl*. New York: Bantam Books, 1993.

Smith, Lyn. *Remembering, Voices of the Holocaust: A New History in the Words of the Men and Women Who Survived*. New York: Carroll & Graf, 2006.

Wiesel, Elie. *Night*. New York: Hill and Wang, 2006.

Zullo, Allan, and Mara Bovsun. *Survivors: True Stories of Children in the Holocaust*. New York: Scholastic, 2004.

Web Links

To learn more about the Holocaust, visit ABDO Publishing Company online at **www.abdopublishing.com**. Web sites about the Holocaust are featured on our Book Links page. These links are routinely monitored and updated to provide the most current information available.

Places To Visit

Museum of Tolerance
9786 West Pico Boulevard
Los Angeles, CA 90035
310-553-8403
www.museumoftolerance.com
Learn what leads people to hate and how ordinary people have changed the world through their extraordinary actions.

National World War II Memorial
17th Street NW/SW between Constitution and Independence Avenues
Washington, DC 20024
202-619-7222
www.wwiimemorial.com
Visit the site that honors the 16 million Americans who served their country during the war, including the more than 400,000 who died.

United States Holocaust Memorial Museum
100 Raoul Wallenberg Place SW
Washington, DC 20024
202-488-0400
www.ushmm.org/visit
Visit the permanent exhibit called The Holocaust and its three sections: Nazi Assault, Final Solution, and Last Chapter.

Glossary

Allies
The group of countries, consisting mainly of the Soviet Union, England, and the United States, that fought against Germany and fellow Axis powers Japan and Italy in World War II.

anti-Semitism
Hatred of Jews.

Aryan
According to Nazi theory, a superior human of Caucasian and Western European ancestry.

concentration camp
A prison used by the Nazis to hold those deemed to be enemies of the state.

death camp
One of the six camps created by the Nazis with the purpose of exterminating prisoners or forcing them into hard labor.

death march
Forced treks of great lengths under brutal conditions used by the Nazis to punish and kill off Jews and others, particularly at the end of the war.

Einsatzgruppen
German death squads that murdered hundreds of thousands of Jews, especially in the Soviet Union.

extermination camps
Six facilities, located mostly in Poland, to which Jews were sent to be murdered through poison gas and other means.

"Final Solution"
The planned extermination of all the Jews in Europe by the Nazi government and the German public.

gas chambers
The large facilities, located in extermination camps, in which Jews and others were killed by poison gas.

genocide
The mass murder of a group of people based on race, religion, ethnicity, or political views.

ghettos
Areas in large cities, particularly in Poland, where Jews were sent to be killed or to await transport to Nazi-run camps.

Holocaust
The systematic murder of an estimated 6 million Jews by the Nazis during World War II.

Kristallnacht
Known in English as the "Night of the Broken Glass," a time of terror for the Jews of Germany on November 9, 1938, in which synagogues were burned down, Jewish businesses were smashed, and many Jews were killed or sent to concentration camps.

Nazi Party
The National Socialist German Workers Party, led by Adolf Hitler, which gained control of the country in 1933 and was responsible for starting World War II and the Holocaust.

Nuremberg Laws
Decrees created by the Nazis in 1935 that defined who was Jewish and set up laws regulating and discriminating against the Jews of Germany.

Schutzstaffel
The SS, or security police, that terrorized Jews and others both in Germany and in the occupied territories during World War II.

synagogue
Jewish place of worship.

Wannsee Conference
A meeting in early 1942, headed by SS leader Reinhard Heydrich, in which the "Final Solution" was coordinated.

Zyklon-B
The hydrogen cyanide gas used to murder Jews at some extermination camps, including Auschwitz.

Source Notes

Chapter 1. Blueprint for Mass Murder
1. Saul Friedländer. *The Years of Extermination: Nazi Germany and the Jews, 1939–1945.* New York: HarperCollins Publishers, 2007. 92.
2. Peter Padfield. *Himmler.* New York: Henry Holt and Company, 1990. 357.
3. Ibid.
4. David Cesarani. *Becoming Eichmann: Rethinking the Life, Crimes, and Trial of a "Desk Murderer."* Rayleigh, Essex, England: De Capo Press, 2006. 197.
5. Saul Friedländer. *The Years of Extermination: Nazi Germany and the Jews, 1939–1945.* New York: HarperCollins Publishers, 2007. 337.
6. Ibid. 338.

Chapter 2. Hitler, Hatred, Prelude to Horror
1. William L. Shirer. *The Rise and Fall of the Third Reich: A History of Nazi Germany.* New York: Simon and Schuster, 1960. 26.
2. David Irving. *The War Path: Hitler's Germany 1933-1939.* New York: Viking Press, 1978. xxi.

Chapter 3. Fanning the Flames
1. William L. Shirer. *The Rise and Fall of the Third Reich: A History of Nazi Germany.* New York: Simon and Schuster, 1960. 241.

Chapter 4. Road of No Return
1. Sir Ivone Kirkpatrick. *The Inner Circle.* New York: Macmillan, 1959. 135.

Chapter 5. Darkness Falls Over Europe
1. Martin Gilbert. *Never Again: A History of the Holocaust.* New York: Universe Publishing, 2000. 66.
2. Ibid. 53.
3. William L. Shirer. *The Rise and Fall of the Third Reich: A History of Nazi Germany.* New York: Simon and Schuster, 1960. 662.

Chapter 6. From Ghettos to Gas
1. William L. Shirer. *The Rise and Fall of the Third Reich: A History of Nazi Germany.* New York: Simon and Schuster, 1960. 971.
2. Ibid.
3. Yehuda Bauer. *A History of the Holocaust.* New York: Franklin Watts, 2001. 247.

Chapter 7. Guinea Pigs and Revenge
1. William L. Shirer. *The Rise and Fall of the Third Reich: A History of Nazi Germany.* New York: Simon and Schuster, 1960. 980.

Source Notes Continued

Chapter 8. The Shocking Discoveries
1. Martin Gilbert. *Never Again: A History of the Holocaust.* New York: Universe Publishing, 2000. 145.
2. Harry J. Herder, Jr. "Liberation of Buchenwald." Remember. org. 20 Sept. 2009 <http://remember.org/witness/herder.html>.
3. Martin Gilbert. *Never Again: A History of the Holocaust.* New York: Universe Publishing, 2000. 152.

Chapter 9. Judgment at Nuremberg
1. Martin Gilbert. *Never Again: A History of the Holocaust.* New York: Universe Publishing, 2000. 161.
2. Ibid. N. pag.

Chapter 10. The Holocaust in History
1. "The Life and Work of Wiesel," Speech delivered by Elie Wiesel in 1995, at the ceremony to mark the 50th anniversary of the liberation of Auschwitz. pbs.org. 21 Sept. 2009 <http://www.pbs. org/eliewiesel/life/auschwitz.html>.
2. Yehuda Bauer. *A History of the Holocaust.* New York: Franklin Watts, 2001. 373.

Index

Index Continued

ABOUT THE AUTHOR

Martin Gitlin was a reporter for two newspapers in northeast Ohio for 20 years before becoming solely a freelance writer. During his two decades as a reporter, Gitlin won more than 40 awards, including first place for general excellence from the Associated Press (AP) in 1995. AP also named him one of the top four features writers in the state of Ohio in 2001. Gitlin has written approximately 20 books about sports and history.

PHOTO CREDITS

AP Images, cover, 1, 8, 18, 30, 33, 34, 42, 44, 48, 52, 62, 69, 79, 80, 84, 87, 96 (top), 96 (bottom), 98 (bottom); Fritz Reiss/ AP Images, 6; Red Line Editorial, Inc., 15, 41; Keystone, Stringer/ Getty Images, 16; David Silverman/Getty Images, 23; Bettmann/ Corbis, 24; File/AP Images, 38, 97; Time Life Pictures/Getty Images, 51, 98 (top); Getty Images, 56; US Army Signal Corps/ AP Images, 61; Margaret Bourke-White/AP Images, 66; Dave Thompson, Press Association/AP Images, 70, 99; Henry L. Griffin/AP Images, 74; Bjoern Sigurdsoen/AP Images, 88; Hasan Sarbakhshian/AP Images, 92; Czarek Sokolowski/AP Images, 95